Four Square

The Personal Writing Coach
for Grades 4-6

Writing and Learning Across the Curriculum

Written by Judith S. Gould & Mary F. Burke
Illustrated by Ginger Illustration

Teaching & Learning Company
a Lorenz company
P.O. Box 802
Dayton, OH 45401-0802

This book belongs to

_____

TLC10447

Table of Contents

Section 1:   My Best Friend.. 9

Section 2:   "Funtertainment".. 17

Section 3:   Party Time.. 25

Section 4:   Hangin' out with Buddies.. 33

Section 5:   Family Fun... 41

Section 6:   Fun on the Road.. 49

Section 7:   Summer Fun... 57

Section 8:   Chillin' Alone... 65

Section 9:   After-School Fun.. 73

Section 10: Teaming Up.. 81

Section 11: Pet Portraits... 89

Section 12: Grown-Up for a Day... 97

Section 13: Fantasy Trip... 105

Dear Teacher or Parent,

A teacher's biggest challenge is time. Between mandatory testing and the test preparation that goes with it and the few resources schools still have, there is precious little time for real instruction. Students with learning and behavioral disabilities bring with them additional challenges to the teaching day. Within any given day in school, there are also interruptions in the flow of instruction that provoke even the most saintly of our profession to near insanity.

Homeschool parent-teachers, we also understand your needs and concerns. Juggling domestic responsibilities and instructional duties is a daunting task. *The Personal Writing Coach* helps streamline instruction so even novice homeschooling parents will find it accessible and easy to use.

Our point is that we know all kinds of teachers and their struggles. The 13 themed units in *The Personal Writing Coach* will work with experienced writing students giving them many opportunities to play with language. *The Personal Writing Coach* will also help your reluctant writers by encouraging them into the process step by step, starting with artwork and progressing gradually to organized pieces of writing.

The process begins with drawing. Meshing the visual with the verbal is a natural first step in writing. It's especially good for reluctant writers who become anxious when it's time to write. Getting them to draw makes the physical action of putting pencil to paper less fearful because it is an already familiar activity.

Listing words in the Word Parade is the next logical progression after the artwork. Even though many children have complete thoughts derived from their artwork, jotting down words is less fearful than having to write full sentences. Some students may not need this activity, but chances are your reluctant writer will.

Repetition with basic and personal vocabulary will give the reluctant writer slow and steady experience with words. For the experienced writer, it provides opportunities to play with words by building on established language skills.

The poetry page is our personal favorite. A variety of poetic forms are included throughout *The Personal Writing Coach*. These help students create a piece of written work using their own words without having to worry about rhyming or meter patterns. These forms are not cast in stone. Teachers are encouraged to change the forms in ways that suit their lessons or add extra craft elements to the writing.

While the coach does not focus on mechanics (spelling, punctuation, grammar) in the activities, writers surely can choose to publish any of the drafts generated in the book in the form of a final, corrected copy.

The four square is a tool to help students who have never used a graphic organizer. We recommend that teachers model the four square and its connection to the actual writing which can be the final piece or just a rough draft. We've included an example on pages vi and vii to help you with your modeling.

This book contains 13 themed units, designed to meet the interests and abilities of your young writers. Each unit brings the prewriting through art, word association, questioning, form poetry, planning and finally composition of prose. Taking the themes through these same steps can help to build writer confidence and fluency.

Sincerely,

Judith   Mary

Judith S. Gould
Mary F. Burke

TLC10447

Dear Writer,

This book is your personal coach for writing. Your writing coach, like a sporting coach is there to give advice and guide you. For each theme in this book, your coach has put together exercises to make your writing stronger. Use the coach to help your thinking and planning. Of course, the writing is up to you. Use your style and make the writing your own.

You can do these themes in any order, but you may find it easier to use the order your coach has provided. You may choose to make final, corrected, gorgeous copies of your writing or you may choose to leave it as a practice or scrimmage. Gear up with trusty pencils, erasers, markers and other sporting equipment and get ready to play!

Sincerely,

Judith   Mary

Judith S. Gould
Mary F. Burke

Four Square

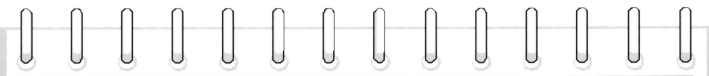

Funny
Makes goofy faces
Scrunches up nose and
crosses eyes
Starts to hiccup
Always makes me laugh when
I feel down

Helpful
Helps me with homework
Math especially
Long division
Before big test spent two hours
helping

Choose one beginning or make up your own:
Best friends are like gold. They're bright, hard to find and valuable to have in your life.
OR
Any day without a best friend is a day without sunshine. My best friend makes every day a great one!

Generous
Always shares
Fruit snack at
lunchbreaks
last potato chip in half
Time
never too busy to talk

Ending
Choose one or
make up your own:
Wouldn't you like
to have a best friend like that?
OR
I have a best friend who is
funny, helpful and generous!
How lucky is that?

That four square now becomes this piece of writing which explains why the writer likes his or her best friend.

Best friends are like gold. They're bright, hard to find and valuable to have in your life. My best friend is all that and more.

To begin with, my best friend Vera is funny. She can make the goofiest faces! The best one is when she scrunches up her nose and crosses her eyes, then she starts to hiccup. Sometimes she'll even read out of our social studies book looking like that. Even when I'm feeling really blue, that goofy face can always make me laugh until my stomach hurts.

Next, Vera is helpful. She always helps me with my homework, especially the dreaded math. Last month when we were learning long division, I thought I was going to go crazy because I couldn't get it. She helped me by explaining every step about a hundred times. Then before our big test in division, she spent two hours with me making sure I was doing all the practice problems right. I got an A on that test, and it was because of all the help I received from her.

Finally, she is really generous. She always shares whatever she has with me. At lunch, half of her fruit snack is always offered to me. Even if she has one potato chip left, she'll split it in half and offer it to me. It's not just food she shares. Vera is very giving with her time. She's never too busy to talk with me, even if she has a pile of work to do.

I have a friend who is funny, helpful and generous! How lucky is that?

Four Square

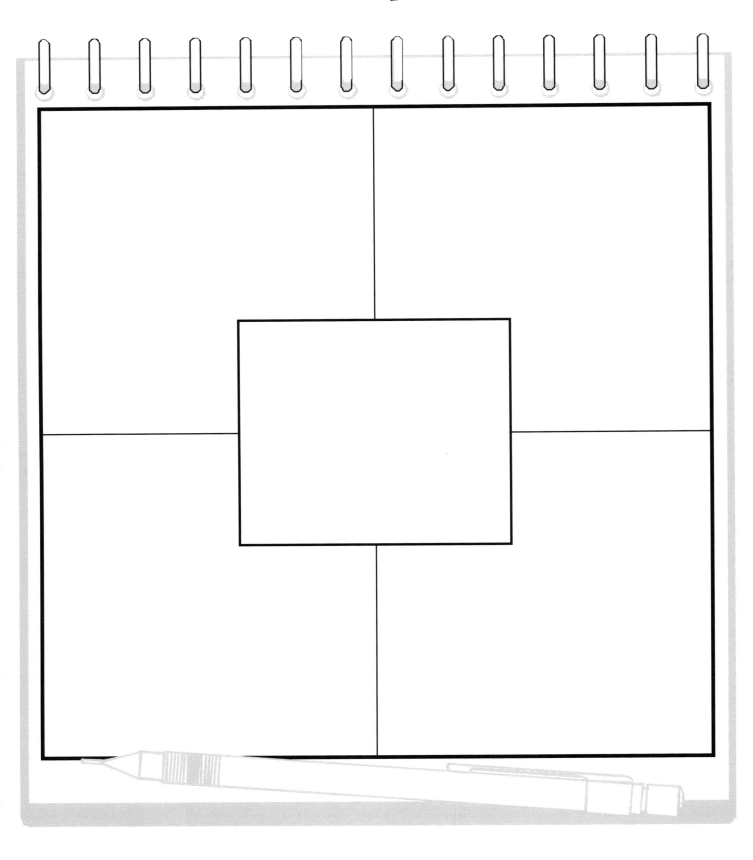

Section 1:
My Best Friend

It is a good idea to have many friends, but usually there are some who are closer than others. Who are your best friends? Is one closer to you than the rest? You will write about the friendships that mean the most to you.

Art to Start

Before you start writing, you have pictures in your head that come first. Let's start with those pictures! Get busy with your markers, colored pencils and crayons. Think about your writing while you are drawing.

Draw a picture of your best friend.

What does your friend like to wear?

Draw one thing that you like to do with your friend.

Word Parade

It's important to have words, and lots of them, parading in front of you before you start to write. Then you can pick them out when you need them. Let's start the parade by listing some words that are already in your head. Don't worry about spelling. You can fix that later.

Words to describe the way your friend looks

Verbs (action words) for the things you do together

Nouns (people, places, things) for the things you talk about together

The places you go together

Huddle Time

If you're getting stuck or see that you are using the same kind of words, try using a thesaurus to help you pump up your word list. The personal writing coach gives a thumbs up to using a thesaurus whenever you write.

Questions and Answers

Your coach would like you to think about your topic by answering these questions. Think of it as interviewing yourself!

1. Who are some of your best friends? _____

   _____

2. What makes them the closest friends? _____

   _____

3. What kinds of things do you do together? _____

   _____

4. Are there some things that you do with your best friend, but not with other friends? _____

   _____

5. When did you start becoming the best of friends? _____

6. Do you ever fight? About what? How long do the fights last? _____

   _____

7. Sometimes friends have special rituals, like a handshake or a pledge. Do you and your friend

   have any of these? Describe them. _____

   _____

8. What would you say is the best thing about your friend? Why? _____

   _____

9. Is there something about your friend that you wish you could change? What? _____

   _____

10. Has there been a time when your friendship was tested? How? What happened? _____

   _____

Poetry

Your coach will help you put your words together to form some poetry. Don't worry, just follow the form and it will be easy and fun.

_____ (name of your friend) *and me*

_____ , _____ , _____ (three things you do together)

_____ _____ (describing words) _____ (friend's name)

_____ (place you go)

_____ _____ (what you talk about)

Together

Here is an example:

> *Mary and me*
> *Writing, eating, talking*
> *Witty crazy Mary*
> *At the bookstore*
> *Stories and music*
> *Together*

Now you try. Just follow the form.

_____

_____

_____

_____

_____

Four Square

This will help organize your thoughts for writing to explain why your best friend is so special. Think of it as a map for your words and ideas so they don't get lost on the way from your head to the paper! In each of the squares, write words or phrases that go with the main idea of each box. Save your sentence writing for later.

One reason why this friend is special:

_____

Details that tell more about this:

1. _____

2. _____

3. _____

An example of something that really happened:

_____

One reason why this friend is special:

_____

Details that tell more about this:

1. _____

2. _____

3. _____

An example of something that really happened:

_____

Choose a beginning:

1. One of my best friends is _____.

2. I love spending time with _____.

3. Where would I be without _____?

One reason why this friend is special:

_____

Details that tell more about this:

1. _____

2. _____

3. _____

An example of something that really happened:

_____

Choose an ending:

1. For all of these reasons, _____ is a great friend.

2. Clearly, I am lucky to have a friend like

_____.

3. _____, a friend for many reasons.

A Word from Your Coach

The phrases and words from your four square will now form sentences for your writing, page 16.

Start with the information in the middle box. Indent that first line on your paper and start writing using the ideas from that box.

When you are done with the middle box, go to the top, left box. Use the ideas and words from that box to form sentences that you will use in your writing. Don't forget to indent when you write these ideas down, because it's a new main idea that forms this new paragraph.

Next go to the top, right box. Use the ideas and words from that box to form sentences that you will use in your writing. Now you're writing about a new idea, so remember to indent. Make sure you add lots of details and interesting words to your sentences to give your writing pizzazz.

As soon as you're done with the top, right box, you will go to the bottom, left box. Use the ideas and words from that box to form sentences that you will use in your writing. New ideas mean another indention for this new paragraph. Make sure your writing sounds like you. Put your personality into it.

The last box is your ending. Even though it's not much writing, it still needs an indention because it's a new idea. You're telling the reader good-bye. Of course, we don't say good-bye, but we try to leave the reader with one last thought or feeling about the topic. Look at your box. What phrases did you write? This will help you with your ending.

Section 2:
"Funtertainment"

Whether we are riding in the car, or just passing sometime hanging around, there are many ways to be entertained. Listening to the radio, going to the movies, getting online or catching a TV show are some popular ways to entertain ourselves with "electronic media." We will think and write about some of the types of entertainment that can fill our idle times.

Art to Start

Before you start writing, you have pictures in your head that come first. Let's start with those pictures! Get busy with your markers, colored pencils and crayons. Think about our writing while you are drawing. Write the name of each person you draw.

Draw a picture that represents your favorite type of music.

Draw your favorite video game or activity on your computer.

Draw something from your favorite movie.

Draw something from your favorite TV program.

TLC10447

Word Parade

It's important to have words, and lots of them, parading in front of you before you start to write. Then you can pick them out when you need them. Let's start the parade by listing some words that are already in your head. Don't worry about spelling. You can fix that later.

Words to describe your favorite kind of music

Verbs (action words) for the things you do with your computer

Nouns (people, places, things) for the things in your favorite movies

Words that tell what kind of TV shows you like to watch

Huddle Time

If you're getting stuck or see that you are using the same kind of words, try using a thesaurus to help you pump up your word list. The personal writing coach gives a thumbs up to using a thesaurus whenever you write.

Questions and Answers

Your coach would like you to think about your topic by answering these questions. Think of it as interviewing yourself!

1. What kind of TV programs are your favorites? Why? Can you name some? _____
   _____

2. What programs do you dislike? Why? _____
   _____

3. What are some programs that you used to like? Why do you think you like them? _____
   _____

4. What music do you listen to most? Can you name a band or radio station you prefer? _____
   _____

5. Why do you like this type of music best? _____
   _____

6. Do you use your computer or the internet? What do you use them for? _____
   _____

7. What are some of your favorite movies? _____
   _____

8. Do you like to go to the movies or rent movies? Why? _____
   _____

9. How often do you watch movies? Watch TV? Listen to music? _____
   _____

10. How do you think your life would be different if you didn't have your music, movies or TV programs?
   _____

Poetry

Your coach will help you put your words together to form some poetry. Don't worry, just follow the form and it will be easy and fun.

_____ (your kind of music) _____ (a sound word to describe it)

It _____, it _____, it _____ (three things it does)

_____ _____ (where or when you listen to it)

_____ (why you listen to it)

This can be used for your favorite TV programs, movies and computer games, too.

Here is an example:

A horror movie, EEK!
It hunts, it captures, it kills
All alone on a dark and stormy night
Scaring myself half to death

Now you try. Just follow the form.

_____

_____

_____

_____

_____

Four Square

This will help organize your thoughts for writing to describe the kinds of entertainment you like best. Think of it as a map for your words and ideas so they don't get lost on the way from your head to the paper! In each of the squares, write words or phrases that go with the main idea of each box. Save your sentence writing for later.

The TV show or movie you like best:

_____

Details about why you like it:

1. _____

2. _____

3. _____

An example of something that really happened in the show:

_____

_____

Music style, band or artist you like best:

_____

Details about why you like it:

1. _____

2. _____

3. _____

An example of something that you like about a favorite song:

_____

_____

Choose a beginning (or use your own):
1. I like many kinds of entertainment.
2. When hanging around, I spend some time with my favorite entertainment.
3. Near my TV, computer or radio I'm never bored.

One thing you like to do on a computer or name a favorite video game:

_____

Details that tell why you like this:

1. _____

2. _____

3. _____

An example of something that is really special about this game, or this use of your computer.

_____

Choose an ending (or use your own):

1. This is why I like _____,

_____ or _____.

2. If I can plug it in, watch it, listen to it and play it, I will always have a fun way to be entertained.

3. I can't wait to watch, listen and play.

A Word from Your Coach

The phrases and words from your four square will now form sentences for your writing, page 24.

Start with the information in the middle box. Indent that first line on your paper and start writing using the ideas from that box.

When you are done with the middle box, go to the top, left box. Use the ideas and words from that box to form sentences that you will use in your writing. Don't forget to indent when you write these ideas down, because it's a new main idea that forms this new paragraph.

Next go to the top, right box. Use the ideas and words from that box to form sentences that you will use in your writing. Now you're writing about a new idea, so remember to indent. Make sure you add lots of details and interesting words to your sentences to give your writing pizzazz.

As soon as you're done with the top, right box, you will go to the bottom, left box. Use the ideas and words from that box to form sentences that you will use in your writing. New ideas mean another indention for this new paragraph. Make sure your writing sounds like you. Put your personality into it.

The last box is your ending. Even though it's not much writing, it still needs an indention because it's a new idea. You're telling the reader good-bye. Of course, we don't say good-bye, but we try to leave the reader with one last thought or feeling about the topic. Look at your box. What phrases did you write? This will help you with your ending.

Party Time

Sometimes we don't need a good reason to have a party. Parties are a great way to get together and just concentrate on fun. Kids and adults use parties to talk, dance and just be together with others. We will write about some of the things that make parties the special times that many look forward to.

Art to Start

Before you start writing, you have pictures in your head that come first. Let's start with those pictures! Get busy with your markers, colored pencils and crayons. Think about our writing while you are drawing.

Draw a picture of a great party place.

Draw a party activity.

Draw a party food.

Draw some of your favorite party guests.

Word Parade

It's important to have words, and lots of them, parading in front of you before you start to write. Then you can pick them out when you need them. Let's start the parade by listing some words that are already in your head. Don't worry about spelling. You can fix that later.

List places where a great party can happen.

Verbs (action words) for the things you do at a great party

Nouns (people, places, things) you need to have a great party

Words that tell what kinds of snacks are at a great party

Huddle Time

If you're getting stuck or see that you are using the same kind of words, try using a thesaurus to help you pump up your word list. The personal writing coach gives a thumbs up to using a thesaurus whenever you write.

Name _____

Questions and Answers

Your coach would like you to think about your topic by answering these questions. Think of it as interviewing yourself!

1. What kinds of parties have you attended recently? Did you like them? _____

   _____

2. What makes a good party? _____

   _____

3. What things do you do at a really good party? Why? _____

   _____

4. Who would you like to see at a great party? Why? _____

   _____

5. What kinds of music will play? Will people dance? How? _____

   _____

6. Do you have parties for "just family"? On what occasions? _____

   _____

7. What kinds of things do you need to do to plan a party? _____

   _____

8. What would you wear to a really great party? _____

   _____

9. What foods or snacks should be at a great party? _____

   _____

Poetry

Your coach will help you put your words together to form some poetry. Don't worry, just follow the form and it will be easy and fun.

Something you do at a party

A sound to go with it

Two words to describe how you do it

Something you eat at a party

A sound to go with it

Two words to describe how you eat it

Something you see at a party

A sound to go with it

Two words to describe how it looks

A great party

Here is an example:

A pillow fight
Swoosh
Slamming, hurling
Buttered popcorn
Munch
Crunching, gulping
Big present pile
"Oh, yes!"
Glittery, decorative
A great party

Now you try. Just follow the form.

_____

_____

_____

_____

_____

_____

_____

_____

Four Square

This will help organize your thoughts for writing to describe a party or celebration. Think of it as a map for your words and ideas so they don't get lost on the way from your head to the paper! In each of the squares, write words or phrases that go with the main idea of each box. Save your sentence writing for later.

The first thing that everyone did at the party:

_____

_____

How did things look? What did you hear? How did you feel?

1. _____

2. _____

3. _____

The party really got cooking when:

_____

_____

How did things look? What did you hear? How did you feel?

1. _____

2. _____

3. _____

Choose a beginning (or use your own):
1. The party was fabulous.
2. Food, friends and fun. What a party.
3. There are many parts to a great party.
4. "Party time!" I shouted. Party day was finally here.

At the end of the party we:

_____

How did things look? What did you hear? How did you feel?

1. _____

2. _____

3. _____

Choose an ending (or use your own):

1. I was so sorry that the party had ended.

2. I will never forget what a great time I had.

3. This was the best party ever.

A Word from Your Coach

The phrases and words from your four square will now form sentences for your writing, page 32.

Start with the information in the middle box. Indent that first line on your paper and start writing using the ideas from that box.

When you are done with the middle box, go to the top, left box. Use the ideas and words from that box to form sentences that you will use in your writing. Don't forget to indent when you write these ideas down, because it's a new main idea that forms this new paragraph.

Next go to the top, right box. Use the ideas and words from that box to form sentences that you will use in your writing. Now you're writing about a new idea, so remember to indent. Make sure you add lots of details and interesting words to your sentences to give your writing pizzazz.

As soon as you're done with the top, right box, you will go to the bottom, left box. Use the ideas and words from that box to form sentences that you will use in your writing. New ideas mean another indention for this new paragraph. Make sure your writing sounds like you. Put your personality into it.

The last box is your ending. Even though it's not much writing, it still needs an indention because it's a new idea. You're telling the reader good-bye. Of course, we don't say good-bye, but we try to leave the reader with one last thought or feeling about the topic. Look at your box. What phrases did you write? This will help you with your ending.

Hangin' out with Buddies

Good friends don't need an amusement park to be amused. Sometimes the best times we can have together are spent just hanging around. Whether we are just inside, being with friends and spending time can be special. We will write about the things to do with friends when nothing special is going on.

Art to Start

Before you start writing, you have pictures in your head that come first. Let's start with those pictures! Get busy with your markers, colored pencils and crayons. Think about your writing while you are drawing.

Draw a picture of a friend who "hangs out" with you.

Draw a place you hang out together.

Draw one thing you do when "hanging out."

Word Parade

It's important to have words, and lots of them, parading in front of you before you start to write. Then you can pick them out when you need them. Let's start the parade by listing some words that are already in your head. Don't worry about spelling. You can fix that later.

List people with whom you hang out.

Verbs (action words) for the things you do together

Nouns (things) you need to hang around

Where you go when hanging out

Huddle Time

If you're getting stuck or see that you are using the same kind of words, try using a thesaurus to help you pump up your word list. The personal writing coach gives a thumbs up to using a thesaurus whenever you write.

Questions and Answers

Your coach would like you to think about your topic by answering these questions. Think of it as interviewing yourself!

1. When do you have time to hang around? Weekdays? Weekends? Summers? _____

   _____

2. Where do you and your buddies hang around mostly? Is it different on different days? In

   different seasons? _____

   _____

3. With whom do you usually "hang around"? Does this change based on season or the school year?

   _____

4. When and how do you and your buddies plan to hang out? How do you decide what you will do

   together? _____

   _____

5. What kinds of things do you do together on a "boring day"? Is this different in different seasons?

   How?_____

   _____

6. Do you use any sports equipment or games when you hang around together?_____

   _____

7. Are there any games that you play? Where do you play them? _____

   _____

8. Do you snack or have something to drink together? What do you have? Who buys it? _____

   _____

9. How long a time do you usually spend together? What time do you start hanging out? When

   does everyone go home? _____

TLC10447

Poetry

Your coach will help you put your words together to form some poetry. Don't worry, just follow the form and it will be easy and fun.

For this poem you will create a recipe of all the things that you need to make hanging out a good time.

Here is the form:

Start with a boring day

Then add a cup full of _____ (people)

Add a tablespoon each of _____ (the things you need)

_____ (the things you do) *and place it in*

_____ (where you go)

End up with a pretty cool day. (Or use your own ending)

Here is an example:

Start with a boring day
Then add a cup full of Deb, Bryce, Evan and Ilana
Add a tablespoon each of chips, dip, movies and craft supplies
Munch, watch and talk in Deb's living room
End up with a pretty cool day.

_____

_____

_____

_____

_____

_____

_____

Four Square

This will help organize your thoughts for writing to explain ways to fill a boring day. Think of it as a map for your words and ideas so they don't get lost on the way from your head to the paper! In each of the squares, write words or phrases that go with the main idea of each box. Save your sentence writing for later.

Where you meet with your friends:

_____

Give three reasons why you meet there. If there are different places at different times, tell why.

1. _____

2. _____

3. _____

The things you need to have:

_____

What equipment will you need? Where will you get these things?

1. _____

2. _____

3. _____

Choose a beginning (or use your own):
1. A boring day doesn't need to stay that way.
2. I'm never really bored if I'm hanging out with my buddies.
3. There are a lot of fun things to do when hanging out with your buddies.

Some of the things you will do:

_____

Use these three details to explain why this will be a fun time for everyone.

1. _____

2. _____

3. _____

Choose an ending (or use your own):

1. If you follow these steps too, you will never be totally bored.

2. As long as we hang around together, we always have a good time.

3. This is how to hang around and have fun with your friends.

A Word from Your Coach

The phrases and words from your four square will now form sentences for your writing, page 40.

Start with the information in the middle box. Indent that first line on your paper and start writing using the ideas from that box.

When you are done with the middle box, go to the top, left box. Use the ideas and words from that box to form sentences that you will use in your writing. Don't forget to indent when you write these ideas down, because it's a new main idea that forms this new paragraph.

Next go to the top, right box. Use the ideas and words from that box to form sentences that you will use in your writing. Now you're writing about a new idea, so remember to indent. Make sure you add lots of details and interesting words to your sentences to give your writing pizzazz.

As soon as you're done with the top, right box, you will go to the bottom, left box. Use the ideas and words from that box to form sentences that you will use in your writing. New ideas mean another indention for this new paragraph. Make sure your writing sounds like you. Put your personality into it.

The last box is your ending. Even though it's not much writing, it still needs an indention because it's a new idea. You're telling the reader good-bye. Of course, we don't say good-bye, but we try to leave the reader with one last thought or feeling about the topic. Look at your box. What phrases did you write? This will help you with your ending.

Section 5:
Family Fun

Yes, your family is made up of your relatives.
But that doesn't mean that you can't enjoy your time together. Even though brothers and sisters fight, they sometimes have fun together. Mom and Dad may make the rules, but sometimes they can laugh and play.
Cousins, aunts, uncles and grandparents can all add to the fun times we enjoy. We will think and write about the times when we have had a blast with our families.

Art to Start

Before you start writing, you have pictures in your head that come first. Let's start with those pictures! Get busy with your markers, colored pencils and crayons. Think about your writing while you are drawing.

Draw something that you enjoy doing with your parents.

Draw something that you enjoy doing with brothers or sisters.

Draw one thing you do with aunts, uncles or grandparents.

Draw one thing you do with cousins.

Word Parade

It's important to have words, and lots of them, parading in front of you before you start to write. Then you can pick them out when you need them. Let's start the parade by listing some words that are already in your head. Don't worry about spelling. You can fix that later.

List the things that you like to do with your family at home.

List the fun things you have done on vacations together.

What words come to mind when you think of time with your grandparents?

List words for the fun things that you do with cousins, aunts or uncles.

Huddle Time

If you're getting stuck or see that you are using the same kind of words, try using a thesaurus to help you pump up your word list. The personal writing coach gives a thumbs up to using a thesaurus whenever you write.

Name _____

Questions and Answers

Your coach would like you to think about your topic by answering these questions. Think of it as interviewing yourself!

1. When does your family have time at home to just "hang around" together? _____

   _____

2. What kinds of things do you like to do with a brother or sister?_____

   _____

3. Does your family have special things to do on long car trips? Lazy Sunday afternoons? What

   do you do? _____

4. Is there something special that you do when spending time with a grandparent? Did they play a

   special game with you when you were little? _____

   _____

5. Sometimes parents are so busy you'd think that they never have fun . . . until you see them on

   vacation. What kinds of things do your parents do on vacation?_____

   _____

6. What kinds of games or sports do you play when spending time together at home? _____

   _____

7. Do you often see your cousins? What do you do together when you see them? _____

   _____

8. Spending time with a grandparent, aunt or uncle can be special because they have permission to

   "spoil" you. What special things can you do with these relatives? _____

   _____

9. What kinds of fun things are done in your house on an everyday basis? Do you tell jokes? Read

   together? Enjoy TV programs and laugh?_____

Name _____

Poetry

Your coach will help you put your words together to form some poetry. Don't worry, just follow the form and it will be easy and fun.

For this one you will create a "5 Ws" poem. To make this form work, just answer these questions about the things you do when you hang around with your family members.

Who do you like to spend time with?
What do you do together?
Where do you do it?
When do you have this time together?
Why is it special?

Here is an example:

> *Bubbe and Great-Grandpa*
> *Cheating at Crazy Eights*
> *While sitting at Bubbe's dining room table*
> *Every time I visit*
> *I love how they let me win*

Now try one on your own.

_____

_____

_____

_____

_____

_____

_____

Four Square

This will help organize your thoughts for writing to describe what you would do with a special family member. Think of it as a map for your words and ideas so they don't get lost on the way from your head to the paper! In each of the squares, write words or phrases that go with the main idea of each box. Save your sentence writing for later.

Where you were with your special person:

_____

Give some details about the setting. Tell about the weather. If it is in a room, describe it with some details.

1. _____

2. _____

3. _____

What is the first thing you did together:

_____

Give some details about each step you took to do this.

1. _____

2. _____

3. _____

Choose a beginning (or use your own):
1. Family time can be as much fun as hanging around with your friends.
2. _____ is the coolest.
Start out by giving a little background. Tell who the person is and when this special time happened.

What is the first thing you did together?

_____

_____

Give some details about each step you took to do this.

1. _____

2. _____

3. _____

Choose an ending (or use your own):

1. I was so sorry that the party had ended.

2. I will never forget what a great time I had.

3. This was the best party ever.

A Word from Your Coach

The phrases and words from your four square will now form sentences for your writing, page 48.

Start with the information in the middle box. Indent that first line on your paper and start writing using the ideas from that box.

When you are done with the middle box, go to the top, left box. Use the ideas and words from that box to form sentences that you will use in your writing. Don't forget to indent when you write these ideas down, because it's a new main idea that forms this new paragraph.

Next go to the top, right box. Use the ideas and words from that box to form sentences that you will use in your writing. Now you're writing about a new idea, so remember to indent. Make sure you add lots of details and interesting words to your sentences to give your writing pizzazz.

As soon as you're done with the top, right box, you will go to the bottom, left box. Use the ideas and words from that box to form sentences that you will use in your writing. New ideas mean another indention for this new paragraph. Make sure your writing sounds like you. Put your personality into it.

The last box is your ending. Even though it's not much writing, it still needs an indention because it's a new idea. You're telling the reader good-bye. Of course, we don't say good-bye, but we try to leave the reader with one last thought or feeling about the topic. Look at your box. What phrases did you write? This will help you with your ending.

Section 6:

Fun on the Road

Traveling can be a lot of work, but it can be fun, too.
Going places can be exiting and getting there is part of the fun.
In this theme we will think and write about some of the places
we would like to go, and the things we will do on the way there.

Art to Start

Before you start writing, you have pictures in your head that come first. Let's start with those pictures! Get busy with your markers, colored pencils and crayons. Think about your writing while you are drawing.

Draw a place that you would like to go.	Draw the way you would go there.

Draw a place that you would like to go.	Draw the way you would go there.

TLC10447

Word Parade

It's important to have words, and lots of them, parading in front of you before you start to write. Then you can pick them out when you need them. Let's start the parade by listing some words that are already in your head. Don't worry about spelling. You can fix that later.

List the places you would like to go.

List the fun things you could do there.

List words that relate to traveling to these places.

List reasons your parents might not want to go there.

Huddle Time

If you're getting stuck or see that you are using the same kind of words, try using a thesaurus to help you pump up your word list. The personal writing coach gives a thumbs up to using a thesaurus whenever you write.

Questions and Answers

Your coach would like you to think about your topic by answering these questions. Think of it as interviewing yourself!

1. What was one of the most special places you have gone as a family? _____
   _____

2. How did you get there? What did you do to have fun along the way? _____
   _____
   _____

3. Are there places you would like to go? Where? Why? _____
   _____

4. What kinds of things will you do at these places? _____
   _____
   _____

5. How will you get to these places? How long will it take? _____
   _____

6. What kinds of things will you do for fun along the way to these places? _____
   _____
   _____

7. What things will there be for your family to do at these places? _____
   _____
   _____

8. How much will it cost to go there? _____
   _____

Poetry

Your coach will help you put your words together to form some poetry. Don't worry, just follow the form and it will be easy and fun.

Three words to describe the place you want to go
Name of the place that you want to go
Three reasons you want to go there
How you would feel on your visit to this place
Use this as many times as you like for each of the places that you would like to go

Here is an example:

Sunny, warm and sandy
Hawaiian Islands
The volcanoes, the luau, hula dancing
A place to relax

Now you try.

_____

_____

_____

_____

_____

_____

_____

Four Square

This will help organize your thoughts for writing to persuade your parents to take you to a special place. Think of it as a map for your words and ideas so they don't get lost on the way from your head to the paper! In each of the squares, write words or phrases that go with the main idea of each box. Save your sentence writing for later.

One reason why you think you should be allowed to go there:

_____

Give some details that explain this reason, or use examples.

1. _____

2. _____

3. _____

Add a specific tidbit to prove it.

One reason why you think you should be allowed to go there:

_____

Give some details that explain this reason, or use examples.

1. _____

2. _____

3. _____

Add a specific tidbit to prove it.

Choose a beginning (or use your own):

1. I really want to visit _____.

2. There are many reasons I should be allowed to go to _____.

3. New places, new faces and new experiences are all available at _____.

One reason why you think you should be allowed to go there:

_____

Give some details that explain this reason, or use examples.

1. _____

2. _____

3. _____

Add a specific tidbit to prove it.

Choose an ending (or use your own):

1. It is clear that this is a great place to go.

2. See? _____ is great. Can we go soon?

3. For all of these reasons, _____ should be the place we plan to go.

A Word from Your Coach

The phrases and words from your four square will now form sentences for your writing, page 56.

Start with the information in the middle box. Indent that first line on your paper and start writing using the ideas from that box.

When you are done with the middle box, go to the top, left box. Use the ideas and words from that box to form sentences that you will use in your writing. Don't forget to indent when you write these ideas down, because it's a new main idea that forms this new paragraph.

Next go to the top, right box. Use the ideas and words from that box to form sentences that you will use in your writing. Now you're writing about a new idea, so remember to indent. Make sure you add lots of details and interesting words to your sentences to give your writing pizzazz.

As soon as you're done with the top, right box, you will go to the bottom, left box. Use the ideas and words from that box to form sentences that you will use in your writing. New ideas mean another indention for this new paragraph. Make sure your writing sounds like you. Put your personality into it.

The last box is your ending. Even though it's not much writing, it still needs an indention because it's a new idea. You're telling the reader good-bye. Of course, we don't say good-bye, but we try to leave the reader with one last thought or feeling about the topic. Look at your box. What phrases did you write? This will help you with your ending.

Section 7:

Summer Fun

Summer is a favorite season for teachers and students alike. Some great memories can be created when filling up those hazy, lazy days. In this theme you will be thinking and writing about those warm and wonderful summer months.

Art to Start

Before you start writing, you have pictures in your head that come first. Let's start with those pictures! Get busy with your markers, colored pencils and crayons. Think about your writing while you are drawing.

Draw something that you enjoy doing in the summer.	Draw something that you can only do in the summer.
Draw one thing you wear in the summer.	Draw one thing you see in the summer only.

TLC10447

Word Parade

It's important to have words, and lots of them, parading in front of you before you start to write. Then you can pick them out when you need them. Let's start the parade by listing some words that are already in your head. Don't worry about spelling. You can fix that later.

How summer looks

How summer feels

Things to do on a summer day

Summer nouns (people, places, things)

Huddle Time

If you're getting stuck or see that you are using the same kind of words, try using a thesaurus to help you pump up your word list. The personal writing coach gives a thumbs up to using a thesaurus whenever you write.

Questions and Answers

Your coach would like you to think about your topic by answering these questions. Think of it as interviewing yourself!

1. What is the best part of summertime? Why is it the best? _____

_____

2. What are the bad parts of summer? _____

_____

3. Do you participate in organized activities in the summer (camp, recreation programs, etc.)?

Do you like these? _____

_____

4. How does your family routine change in the summertime? _____

_____

5. Do you do different things with your friends in the summer? What do you do? _____

_____

6. How does your neighborhood look and feel in the summer? How is it different from the rest of

the year? _____

_____

7. What are your favorite summer activities? _____

_____

_____

8. How do you dress in summer? How is it different from the rest of the year? _____

_____

_____

Name _____

Poetry

Your coach will help you put your words together to form some poetry. Don't worry, just follow the form and it will be easy and fun.

In this poetry form we will try using some alliteration. This is a poetic affect that many writers use to create an image in writing. Don't worry, your coach will make it easy.

First decide on a letter. We'll use "B" for our example. Now think of a few "B" words about summer: backyard, barbecue, baseball.

Repeat this activity for the next two letters in the alphabet.

C-collect, caterpillars, cousin

D-design, delicious, dessert

End line-This is summer!

Here is an example:

> Backyard barbecuing and tossing the baseball
> Collecting caterpillars with my cousins
> Designing delicious ice cream sundaes for dessert
> This is summer!

Now you try.

Letter: _____ Words: _____, _____, _____

Letter: _____ Words: _____, _____, _____

Letter: _____ Words: _____, _____, _____

Put it together here.

_____

_____

_____

_____

Name _____

Four Square

This will help organize your thoughts for writing to explain why summer is a great time of year. Think of it as a map for your words and ideas so they don't get lost on the way from your head to the paper! In each of the squares, write words or phrases that go with the main idea of each box. Save your sentence writing for later.

A reason that summer is best:

_____

Give some details that explain this reason, or use examples.

1. _____
2. _____
3. _____

Add a real-life example to prove it.

A reason that summer is best:

_____

Give some details that explain this reason, or use examples.

1. _____
2. _____
3. _____

Add a real-life example to prove it.

Choose a beginning (or use your own):
1. Summer is a great time of year.
2. I wish the summer could last all year.
3. June, July and August are the months I like best.
4. You can keep the other seasons. Give me the summertime.

A reason that summer is best: _____

_____

Give some details that explain this reason, or use examples.

1. _____
2. _____
3. _____

Add a real-life example to prove it.

Choose an ending (or use your own):

1. These are some of the reasons that I wish that the summer could last all year.

2. I can't wait for summer!

3. Summer sunshine and summer fun make me one happy kid.

TLC10447

A Word from Your Coach

The phrases and words from your four square will now form sentences for your writing, page 64.

Start with the information in the middle box. Indent that first line on your paper and start writing using the ideas from that box.

When you are done with the middle box, go to the top, left box. Use the ideas and words from that box to form sentences that you will use in your writing. Don't forget to indent when you write these ideas down, because it's a new main idea that forms this new paragraph.

Next go to the top, right box. Use the ideas and words from that box to form sentences that you will use in your writing. Now you're writing about a new idea, so remember to indent. Make sure you add lots of details and interesting words to your sentences to give your writing pizzazz.

As soon as you're done with the top, right box, you will go to the bottom, left box. Use the ideas and words from that box to form sentences that you will use in your writing. New ideas mean another indention for this new paragraph. Make sure your writing sounds like you. Put your personality into it.

The last box is your ending. Even though it's not much writing, it still needs an indention because it's a new idea. You're telling the reader good-bye. Of course, we don't say good-bye, but we try to leave the reader with one last thought or feeling about the topic. Look at your box. What phrases did you write? This will help you with your ending.

Section 8:

Chillin' Alone

Just because none of your friends can come over, it doesn't mean that you have to be totally bored. There are many things that people do to enjoy their time alone. In this theme you will think and write about the times you are busy but alone.

Art to Start

Before you start writing, you have pictures in your head that come first. Let's start with those pictures! Get busy with your markers, colored pencils and crayons. Think about your writing while you are drawing.

Draw the place where you
are most likely to spend time alone.

Draw something that you
only do when you are spending a day alone.

Draw things that you only use when you are spending time alone.

Word Parade

It's important to have words, and lots of them, parading in front of you before you start to write. Then you can pick them out when you need them. Let's start the parade by listing some words that are already in your head. Don't worry about spelling. You can fix that later.

Things I think about when I am alone

How I feel when spending time alone

Things I do when spending time alone

Nouns (places, things) that you see or use during your time alone

Huddle Time

If you're getting stuck or see that you are using the same kind of words, try using a thesaurus to help you pump up your word list. The personal writing coach gives a thumbs up to using a thesaurus whenever you write.

Questions and Answers

Your coach would like you to think about your topic by answering these questions. Think of it as interviewing yourself!

1. Do you like spending time alone? Why or why not? _____

   _____

2. Where are you most likely to spend sometime alone? _____

3. Are there things that you prefer to do alone? What are they? Why do you prefer to be alone?

   _____

4. When are you most likely to spend time by yourself? _____

   _____

5. When spending time alone, do you prefer quiet? If not, what noises do you like to hear? Music?

   The TV? _____

   _____

6. When spending time alone, many people lapse into thoughts. What kinds of things do you like to

   think about when you have some time by yourself? _____

   _____

7. Is there a little time every day that you have some alone time? What do you do during that time?

   _____

   _____

8. Do your family members like to have time alone? How do you feel when they ask you to give them

   some alone time? _____

   _____

Poetry

Your coach will help you put your words together to form some poetry. Don't worry, just follow the form and it will be easy and fun.

When I am alone I'm not by myself

I have my _____ (one or more things you use) to keep me company

Together we _____ (something you do together)

All by myself _____ (where you are)

End with a statement of how you feel during your time alone.

Here is an example:

> When I'm alone I'm not by myself
> I have my book and my kitty to keep me company
> Together we snuggle and escape into fantasy and fiction
> All by myself in my favorite chair
> I feel like I am in heaven

Now you try.

_____

_____

_____

_____

_____

_____

_____

_____

Four Square

This will help organize your thoughts for writing to explain things you like to do by yourself. Think of it as a map for your words and ideas so they don't get lost on the way from your head to the paper! In each of the squares, write words or phrases that go with the main idea of each box. Save your sentence writing for later.

Where you like to go when you can be alone:

_____

Use details that tells what you like best about the place.

1. _____

2. _____

3. _____

Add a detail that tells what you like best about the place.

One thing that you like to do alone:

_____

Explain how you do it.

1. _____

2. _____

3. _____

Add an example that describes the way you did this last time.

Choose a beginning (or use your own):
1. By myself I can do a lot of things to keep from being bored.
2. Sometimes I can be my own best friend.
3. If my buddies are busy, I'm not worried. I like spending time hangin' by myself.

How you feel spending time doing this: _____

_____

Give some details that tell the kinds of things you think about when doing this.

1. _____

2. _____

3. _____

Choose an ending (or use your own):

1. Alone, by myself, is some of the best time I have.

2. While I will always enjoy hangin' with my buddies, being alone can be a good time, too.

3. This is how I spend my time alone.

A Word from Your Coach

The phrases and words from your four square will now form sentences for your writing, page 72.

Start with the information in the middle box. Indent that first line on your paper and start writing using the ideas from that box.

When you are done with the middle box, go to the top, left box. Use the ideas and words from that box to form sentences that you will use in your writing. Don't forget to indent when you write these ideas down, because it's a new main idea that forms this new paragraph.

Next go to the top, right box. Use the ideas and words from that box to form sentences that you will use in your writing. Now you're writing about a new idea, so remember to indent. Make sure you add lots of details and interesting words to your sentences to give your writing pizzazz.

As soon as you're done with the top, right box, you will go to the bottom, left box. Use the ideas and words from that box to form sentences that you will use in your writing. New ideas mean another indention for this new paragraph. Make sure your writing sounds like you. Put your personality into it.

The last box is your ending. Even though it's not much writing, it still needs an indention because it's a new idea. You're telling the reader good-bye. Of course, we don't say good-bye, but we try to leave the reader with one last thought or feeling about the topic. Look at your box. What phrases did you write? This will help you with your ending.

Section 9:
After-School Fun

Parties, road trips and summertime are all fun.
But we can't limit our good times to only those occasions!
Even though the after-school hours usually include homework
and chores, many days we can still squeeze in a little fun.
In this theme you will think and write about
the ways you can have fun every day.

Art to Start

Before you start writing, you have pictures in your head that come first. Let's start with those pictures! Get busy with your markers, colored pencils and crayons. Think about your writing while you are drawing.

Draw one thing you enjoy doing every day.

Draw something you sometimes do after school.

Sketch a picture to show the fun after-school activities you do.

TLC10447

Word Parade

It's important to have words, and lots of them, parading in front of you before you start to write. Then you can pick them out when you need them. Let's start the parade by listing some words that are already in your head. Don't worry about spelling. You can fix that later.

Things I have to do after school

Things I would like to do after school

Places I go after school

People I see after school

Huddle Time

If you're getting stuck or see that you are using the same kind of words, try using a thesaurus to help you pump up your word list. The personal writing coach gives a thumbs up to using a thesaurus whenever you write.

Name _____

Questions and Answers

Your coach would like you to think about your topic by answering these questions. Think of it as interviewing yourself!

1. Where do you go right after school ends? Home? To a sitter? A neighbor? _____
   _____

2. Is it homework first, or do you get a bit of time to unwind? _____
   _____

3. What other kids do you see during the after-school times?_____
   _____

4. What do you do together? _____
   _____

5. Do you grab an after-school snack? What do you like?_____
   _____

6. Are you a part of any activities (Scouts, band, chorus, sports, drama, church groups) that

   meet in the after-school hours? _____

   _____

   _____

7. Do you enjoy these after-school activities? _____
   _____

8. Do you sometimes find it tough to squeeze in fun time with all of your responsibilities

   (homework, chores)? How do you manage? _____

   _____

   _____

TLC10447

Poetry

Your coach will help you put your words together to form some poetry. Don't worry, just follow the form and it will be easy and fun.

This poem will be a comparison of during and after school. Just follow the form.

During school I see _____

After school it's _____ (something you see)

During school I hear _____

After school it's _____ (something you hear)

During school I _____ (something you do)

After school it's _____ (something you do)

During school I feel _____

After school it's _____

Here is an example:

During school I see papers and pencils
After school it's skateboards and ramps
During school I hear "inside voices"
After school I shout
During school I work all day
After school it's play
During school I feel a little stressed
After school I go wild

Now you try.

_____

_____

_____

_____

_____

_____

_____

Four Square

This will help organize your thoughts for writing to describe the things you like to do after school. Think of it as a map for your words and ideas so they don't get lost on the way from your head to the paper! In each of the squares, write words or phrases that go with the main idea of each box. Save your sentence writing for later.

Where you like to go after school?

_____

Use details to describe the place.

1. _____
2. _____
3. _____

Add detail that tells what you like best about the place.

Who do you see after school?

_____

Name the people, and tell something about each of them.

1. _____
2. _____
3. _____

Choose a beginning (or use your own):
1. When school is out, I'm ready for some fun!
2. Rrring! That was the dismissal bell. I'm ready to play.
3. I do many things for fun after school.

Some of the things that you do together:

_____

_____

Give some details about how you do it and why you like doing it.

1. _____
2. _____
3. _____

Choose an ending (or use your own):

1. Homework and chores are fine for some, but I like to have fun after school.

2. After school, at _____ (place),

   with _____ (person), I can have a good time.

3. This is how I spend my time after school.

A Word From Your Coach

The phrases and words from your four square will now form sentences for your writing, page 80.

Start with the information in the middle box. Indent that first line on your paper and start writing using the ideas from that box.

When you are done with the middle box, go to the top, left box. Use the ideas and words from that box to form sentences that you will use in your writing. Don't forget to indent when you write these ideas down, because it's a new main idea that forms this new paragraph.

Next go to the top, right box. Use the ideas and words from that box to form sentences that you will use in your writing. Now you're writing about a new idea, so remember to indent. Make sure you add lots of details and interesting words to your sentences to give your writing pizzazz.

As soon as you're done with the top, right box, you will go to the bottom, left box. Use the ideas and words from that box to form sentences that you will use in your writing. New ideas mean another indention for this new paragraph. Make sure your writing sounds like you. Put your personality into it.

The last box is your ending. Even though it's not much writing, it still needs an indention because it's a new idea. You're telling the reader good-bye. Of course, we don't say good-bye, but we try to leave the reader with one last thought or feeling about the topic. Look at your box. What phrases did you write? This will help you with your ending.

Section 10:

Teaming Up

Whether a member of an official team or playing around with
a ball outside the house, sports seem to be a part of life.
There are so many sports to choose from:
swimming, football, downhill skiing, tennis, hockey–
sports give people a great way to have fun and stay fit.
In this theme you will think and write about some of the
sports you play or would you like to play.

Art to Start

Before you start writing, you have pictures in your head that come first. Let's start with those pictures! Get busy with your markers, colored pencils and crayons. Think about your writing while you are drawing.

Draw one team sport that you watch or play.

Draw an individual sport that you watch or play.

Sketch a sport that you wish to play one day.

Make a sketch representing a local or a favorite sports team.

Word Parade

It's important to have words, and lots of them, parading in front of you before you start to write. Then you can pick them out when you need them. Let's start the parade by listing some words that are already in your head. Don't worry about spelling. You can fix that later.

Name one sport you play. _____ Now list the words that go with it.

Name one sport you play or wish to play. _____
Now list the words that go with it.

Name one sport you play or wish to play. _____
Now list the words that go with it.

Name one sport you play or wish to play. _____
Now list the words that go with it.

Huddle Time

If you're getting stuck or see that you are using the same kind of words, try using a thesaurus to help you pump up your word list. The personal writing coach gives a thumbs up to using a thesaurus whenever you write.

Questions and Answers

Your coach would like you to think about your topic by answering these questions. Think of it as interviewing yourself!

1. Are you now, or have you ever been, a member of a sports team? What sport? _____

   _____

2. What would you say is your favorite part of that sport? What did you dislike? _____

   _____

   _____

3. Do you play any informal sports or games? Which ones? Where do you play? _____

   _____

   _____

4. What are the individual sports that you do (biking, in-line skating, running, etc.)? What do you

   like about these sports?_____

   _____

5. Do you watch any professional or college level sports or games? Which ones? What do you like

   about these sports? _____

   _____

6. Are you a fan of a team or some teams? Which ones? Why are you a fan? Does your whole

   family root for that team? _____

   _____

   _____

7. Is there a sport that you would like to play some day? Which one? Why? _____

   _____

TLC10447

Poetry

Your coach will help you put your words together to form some poetry. Don't worry, just follow the form and it will be easy and fun.

When I get out in the _____ (place your sport happens)

I _____ _____ _____ (what you do)

Just give me my _____ (a piece of equipment you use)

And my _____ (another piece of equipment)

And watch me _____

Here is an example:

> When I get out in the alley
> I concentrate, aim and shoot
> Just give me my hammer bowling ball
> And my trusty band
> And watch me throw a strike

Now you try.

_____

_____

_____

_____

_____

Four Square

This will help organize your thoughts for writing a story about your favorite sport. Think of it as a map for your words and ideas so they don't get lost on the way from your head to the paper! In each of the squares, write words or phrases that go with the main idea of each box. Save your sentence writing for later.

Something goes wrong in the game:

_____

Use details to describe what you see, hear and feel.

1. _____
2. _____
3. _____

What do you try to do?

_____

Use details to describe what you see, hear and feel.

1. _____
2. _____
3. _____

Choose a beginning (or use your own):

1. _____ is the greatest sport.
2. I love playing _____.

Now give a little background. Who is playing? Where and when are you playing?

How do you overcome the problem?

_____

_____

Use details to describe what you see, hear and feel.

1. _____
2. _____
3. _____

How did life go on afterwards? Describe with details about what you saw, felt and heard after the game ended.

A Word from Your Coach

The phrases and words from your four square will now form sentences for your writing, page 88.

Start with the information in the middle box. Indent that first line on your paper and start writing using the ideas from that box.

When you are done with the middle box, go to the top, left box. Use the ideas and words from that box to form sentences that you will use in your writing. Don't forget to indent when you write these ideas down, because it's a new main idea that forms this new paragraph.

Next go to the top, right box. Use the ideas and words from that box to form sentences that you will use in your writing. Now you're writing about a new idea, so remember to indent. Make sure you add lots of details and interesting words to your sentences to give your writing pizzazz.

As soon as you're done with the top, right box, you will go to the bottom, left box. Use the ideas and words from that box to form sentences that you will use in your writing. New ideas mean another indention for this new paragraph. Make sure your writing sounds like you. Put your personality into it.

The last box is your ending. Even though it's not much writing, it still needs an indention because it's a new idea. You're telling the reader good-bye. Of course, we don't say good-bye, but we try to leave the reader with one last thought or feeling about the topic. Look at your box. What phrases did you write? This will help you with your ending.

Section 11:
Pet Portraits

Having a pet can be the best thing in the world!
Having an animal around can be lots of fun and it can also
teach you a lot of things about yourself!
Let's get ready to think all about pets!

Art to Start

Before you start writing, you have pictures in your head that come first. Let's start with those pictures! Get busy with your markers, colored pencils and crayons. Think about your writing while you are drawing.

Draw a picture of a pet you have or would like to have.	Draw a picture of you feeding this pet.
Draw a picture of you and your pet on a typical day with each other.	Draw a picture of how you would entertain your pet.

Word Parade

It's important to have words, and lots of them, parading in front of you before you start to write. Then you can pick them out when you need them. Let's start the parade by listing some words that are already in your head. Don't worry about spelling. You can fix that later.

List creatures you'd like as pets. Circle one as your favorite.	**Choose possible pet names for the pet you circled.**
Choose five words that describe your pet's size.	**Choose five words that describe how your pet feels when you touch it.**

Choose five words that describe how your pet moves.

Huddle Time

If you're getting stuck or see that you are using the same kind of words, try using a thesaurus to help you pump up your word list. The personal writing coach gives a thumbs up to using a thesaurus whenever you write.

Name _____

Questions and Answers

Your coach would like you to think about your topic by answering these questions. Think of it as interviewing yourself!

1. What kind of pet do you have or would you like to have? _____

2. Why is this animal your #1 choice? _____

   _____

3. What kind of things would you create for this animal? _____

   _____

4. What kinds of things would you do to care for your pet? _____

   _____

5. How would you entertain your pet? _____

   _____

6. How would your pet entertain you? _____

   _____

7. What do you think are the most important responsibilities about being a pet owner? _____

   _____

   _____

8. What do you think will be the things that will be easy to do for your pet? Why? _____

   _____

9. What things do you think will be the most difficult? Why? _____

   _____

10. Does your pet have a name? What is it? Why did you choose that particular name? _____

   _____

TLC10447

Poetry

This poem form is very easy because you are just using your own words, exactly the way you talk, to make the poem. Not all poems rhyme, so it's okay if yours doesn't, but it's also just fine if you write it so it rhymes.

It starts with these words:
The best thing about my
Pet is _____

_____.

It _____ and
(action word here)

_____
(action word here)

_____
(Tell where it does these actions)

Here is an example:

The best thing about my
Cat, Mr. Kitty, is that
He's round and
Plump and orange.

He snores and snoozes
In my dad's favorite
Chair and won't move
Even when my dad
Tries to sit on him.

_____

_____

_____

_____

_____

_____

_____

_____

Name _____

Four Square

This will help organize your thoughts for writing to describe your special pet. Think of it as a map for your words and ideas so they don't get lost on the way from your head to the paper! In each of the squares, write words or phrases that go with the main idea of each box. Save your sentence writing for later.

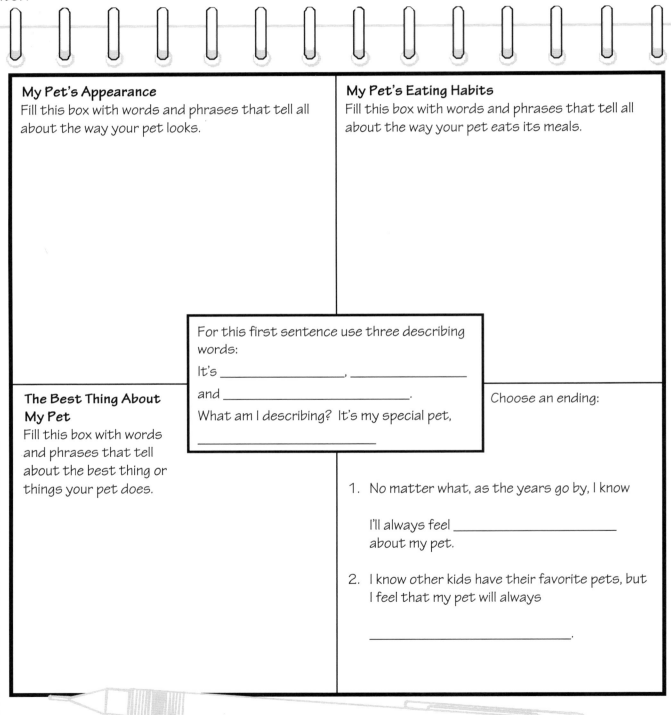

My Pet's Appearance
Fill this box with words and phrases that tell all about the way your pet looks.

My Pet's Eating Habits
Fill this box with words and phrases that tell all about the way your pet eats its meals.

For this first sentence use three describing words:
It's _____, _____
and _____.
What am I describing? It's my special pet,
_____

The Best Thing About My Pet
Fill this box with words and phrases that tell about the best thing or things your pet does.

Choose an ending:

1. No matter what, as the years go by, I know

   I'll always feel _____
   about my pet.

2. I know other kids have their favorite pets, but I feel that my pet will always

   _____.

TLC10447

A Word from Your Coach

The phrases and words from your four square will now form sentences for your writing, page 96.

Start with the information in the middle box. Indent that first line on your paper and start writing using the ideas from that box.

When you are done with the middle box, go to the top, left box. Use the ideas and words from that box to form sentences that you will use in your writing. Don't forget to indent when you write these ideas down, because it's a new main idea that forms this new paragraph.

Next go to the top, right box. Use the ideas and words from that box to form sentences that you will use in your writing. Now you're writing about a new idea, so remember to indent. Make sure you add lots of details and interesting words to your sentences to give your writing pizzazz.

As soon as you're done with the top, right box, you will go to the bottom, left box. Use the ideas and words from that box to form sentences that you will use in your writing. New ideas mean another indention for this new paragraph. Make sure your writing sounds like you. Put your personality into it.

The last box is your ending. Even though it's not much writing, it still needs an indention because it's a new idea. You're telling the reader good-bye. Of course, we don't say good-bye, but we try to leave the reader with one last thought or feeling about the topic. Look at your box. What phrases did you write? This will help you with your ending.

Section 12:
Grown-Up for a Day

Sometimes being a kid can be a real pain!
Everyone tells you what to do!
Wouldn't it be nice to be a grown-up just for a day?
We're going to think about it a lot before we write!

Art to Start

Before you start writing, you have pictures in your head that come first. Let's start with those pictures! Get busy with your markers, colored pencils and crayons. Think about your writing while you are drawing.

Draw what you think you'll
look like when you're a grown-up.

Draw yourself as a
grown-up doing a special job.

Draw yourself as a grown-up doing
something with your grown-up friends.

Draw yourself as a grown-up doing
something special in the evening.

TLC10447

Word Parade

It's important to have words, and lots of them, parading in front of you before you start to write. Then you can pick them out when you need them. Let's start the parade by listing some words that are already in your head. Don't worry about spelling. You can fix that later.

Words that describe your looks as a grown-up

Action words that describe your typical day as a grown-up

Adjectives that describe being a grown-up for a day

Things that you would have as a grown-up

Huddle Time

If you're getting stuck or see that you are using the same kind of words, try using a thesaurus to help you pump up your word list. The personal writing coach gives a thumbs up to using a thesaurus whenever you write.

Questions and Answers

Your coach would like you to think about your topic by answering these questions. Think of it as interviewing yourself!

1. What age do you consider to be the perfect grown-up age? Why? _____

   _____

2. If you were this particular age, what do you think you'd look like? _____

   _____

3. What kind of job would you have? _____

   _____

4. How would you start your day as a grown-up? _____

   _____

5. How would you spend your evenings? _____

   _____

6. What kinds of things would you do with your friends? _____

   _____

7. What kinds of things would you eat as a grown-up? _____

   _____

8. What do you think would be the best thing about spending a day as a grown-up? _____

   _____

9. What do you think would be the worst thing about a day as a grown-up?_____

   _____

10. What kind of grown-up would you pattern yourself after? _____

   _____

Poetry

Writing isn't always about a story. Poems are a great way of getting your feeling down in a shorter way. Don't panic! Poems are fun and remember they don't always have to rhyme! In fact, this one doesn't rhyme unless you want it to.

Here is an example:

In twenty years
I'll look in the mirror
And see _____ .

In twenty years
I'll look in the mirror
And see someone really old.

Every morning I'll wake up
And _____
And every afternoon I'll
Come home to
_____
_____ .

Every morning I'll wake up
And ache because my bones
    Will be so old
And every afternoon I'll
Come home to
My dog Puma who will
Bring me my slippers.

I'll be _____
And _____
And always _____
And I'll never _____
But sometimes I might
_____ .

I'll be working
And I'll never go to bed early
And always I'll have pancakes
    For dinner
And I'll never eat vegetables
But sometimes I might have salad.

In twenty years
I will definitely be
_____
_____ .

In twenty years
I will definitely be
Ready to get my own car.

Name _____

Four Square

This will help organize your thoughts for writing to explain what you would do if you were a grown-up for a day. Think of it as a map for your words and ideas so they don't get lost on the way from your head to the paper! In each of the squares, write words or phrases that go with the main idea of each box. Save your sentence writing for later.

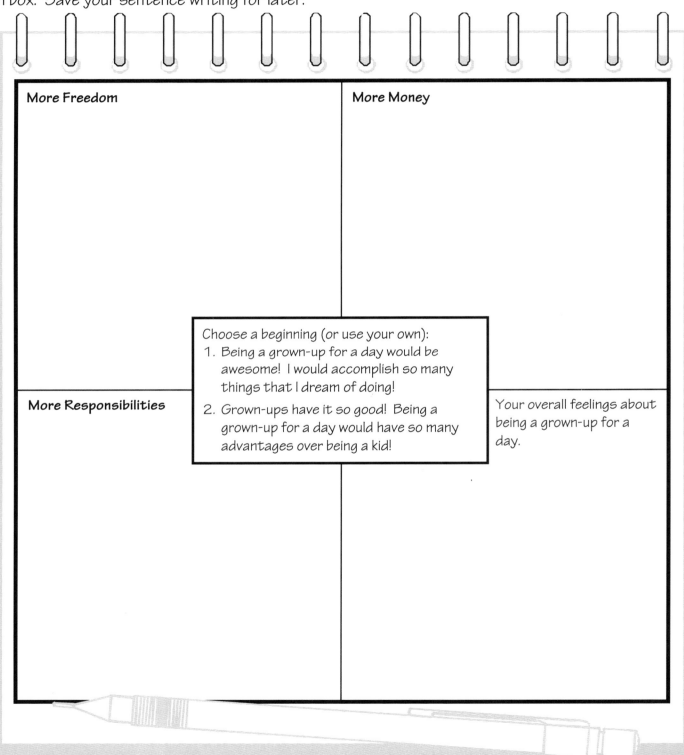

More Freedom

More Money

More Responsibilities

Choose a beginning (or use your own):
1. Being a grown-up for a day would be awesome! I would accomplish so many things that I dream of doing!
2. Grown-ups have it so good! Being a grown-up for a day would have so many advantages over being a kid!

Your overall feelings about being a grown-up for a day.

TLC10447

A Word from Your Coach

The phrases and words from your four square will now form sentences for your writing, page 104.

Start with the information in the middle box. Indent that first line on your paper and start writing using the ideas from that box.

When you are done with the middle box, go to the top, left box. Use the ideas and words from that box to form sentences that you will use in your writing. Don't forget to indent when you write these ideas down, because it's a new main idea that forms this new paragraph.

Next go to the top, right box. Use the ideas and words from that box to form sentences that you will use in your writing. Now you're writing about a new idea, so remember to indent. Make sure you add lots of details and interesting words to your sentences to give your writing pizzazz.

As soon as you're done with the top, right box, you will go to the bottom, left box. Use the ideas and words from that box to form sentences that you will use in your writing. New ideas mean another indention for this new paragraph. Make sure your writing sounds like you. Put your personality into it.

The last box is your ending. Even though it's not much writing, it still needs an indention because it's a new idea. You're telling the reader good-bye. Of course, we don't say good-bye, but we try to leave the reader with one last thought or feeling about the topic. Look at your box. What phrases did you write? This will help you with your ending.

Section 13:

Fantasy Trip

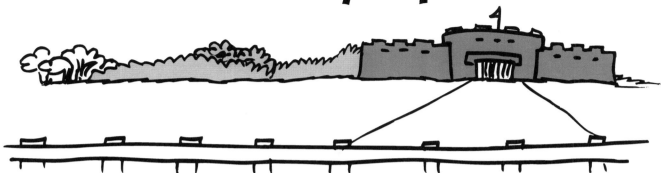

Do you have a place you've never visited but have always wanted to go? It could be a place you've read about that's far away. It could be somewhere closer to you that has always made you curious. Think about it because, we're going to take you there with your writing! Ready? Here we go!

Art to Start

Before you start writing, you have pictures in your head that come first. Let's start with those pictures! Get busy with your markers, colored pencils and crayons. Think about your writing while you are drawing.

Draw your fantasy location.

Draw one thing you'd do there.

Draw who would accompany you to this place.

Draw what you'll eat there.

TLC10447

Word Parade

It's important to have words, and lots of them, parading in front of you before you start to write. Then you can pick them out when you need them. Let's start the parade by listing some words that are already in your head. Don't worry about spelling. You can fix that later.

List words that describe this special place.

Write words that tell what you'd do once you get there.

Write the names of things you'd see there.

List words that describe how you'll feel there.

Huddle Time

If you're getting stuck or see that you are using the same kind of words, try using a thesaurus to help you pump up your word list. The personal writing coach gives a thumbs up to using a thesaurus whenever you write.

Questions and Answers

Your coach would like you to think about your topic by answering these questions. Think of it as interviewing yourself!

1. Where will your fantasy trip take you? _____

2. Why did you choose this place? _____

   _____

3. How will you get to this special place? _____

   _____

4. In your fantasy, how long will you stay there? Why will you stay there that amount of time?

   _____

   _____

5. What's the first thing you'll do when you get there? _____

   _____

6. Who will go with you? Why did you choose these particular friends? _____

   _____

7. What will you photograph while you are there? Why? _____

   _____

8. After this fantasy trip is completed, what do you think you'll remember most about it?

   _____

   _____

Poetry

Writing isn't always about a story. Poems are a great way of getting your feelings down in a shorter way. Don't panic! Poems are fun and remember, they don't always have to rhyme! In fact, this one doesn't rhyme unless you want it to.

Here is how to do it:

Write two words that describe this place.
Name of place
I can't wait to
verb and detail
verb and detail
verb and detail
verb and detail
verb and detail
A phrase that tells how you feel

Here is an example:

Warm, beautiful
Atlantic Beach
I can't wait to
snooze under a palm tree
splash in the cool ocean
build a giant sand castle
dig up seashells
dive under giant waves
I hope I never leave!

_____

_____

_____

_____

_____

_____

_____

Name _____

Four Square

This will help organize your thoughts for writing to describe your special fantasy trip. Think of it as a map for your words and ideas so they don't get lost on the way from your head to the paper! In each of the squares, write words or phrases that go with the main idea of each box. Save your sentence writing for later.

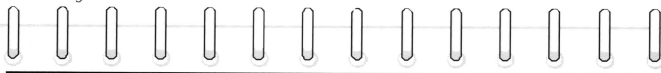

Who will go with you?

Fill this box with the details about who will go with you and why they are the best people to take on this very special trip. If you are going alone, tell why you've chosen to go alone.

What will you do there?

Fill this box with words and phrases all about the things you'll do once you arrive. Use as many specific details as you can.

For this first sentence use three describing words:

It's _____, _____

and _____. What am I

describing? It's my special fantasy trip,

_____.

What will you photograph or record while you are there?

Fill this box with words and phrases about the things you will record while you are there. What's so special about these things that make you want to record them to take with you?

Choose an ending:

I know it's just a fantasy now, but one day I

really hope to visit _____.

OR

Just thinking about _____
always makes me feel better even if I'm having a bad day!

TLC10447

A Word from Your Coach

The phrases and words from your four square will now form sentences for your writing, page 112.

Start with the information in the middle box. Indent that first line on your paper and start writing using the ideas from that box.

When you are done with the middle box, go to the top, left box. Use the ideas and words from that box to form sentences that you will use in your writing. Don't forget to indent when you write these ideas down, because it's a new main idea that forms this new paragraph.

Next go to the top, right box. Use the ideas and words from that box to form sentences that you will use in your writing. Now you're writing about a new idea, so remember to indent. Make sure you add lots of details and interesting words to your sentences to give your writing pizzazz.

As soon as you're done with the top, right box, you will go to the bottom, left box. Use the ideas and words from that box to form sentences that you will use in your writing. New ideas mean another indention for this new paragraph. Make sure your writing sounds like you. Put your personality into it.

The last box is your ending. Even though it's not much writing, it still needs an indention because it's a new idea. You're telling the reader good-bye. Of course, we don't say good-bye, but we try to leave the reader with one last thought or feeling about the topic. Look at your box. What phrases did you write? This will help you with your ending.